Australia
For Kids
People, Places and Cultures
Children Explore The World Books

BABY PROFESSOR
EDUCATION KIDS

Speedy Publishing LLC
40 E. Main St. #1156
Newark, DE 19711
www.speedypublishing.com

Let's learn some interesting facts about Australia!

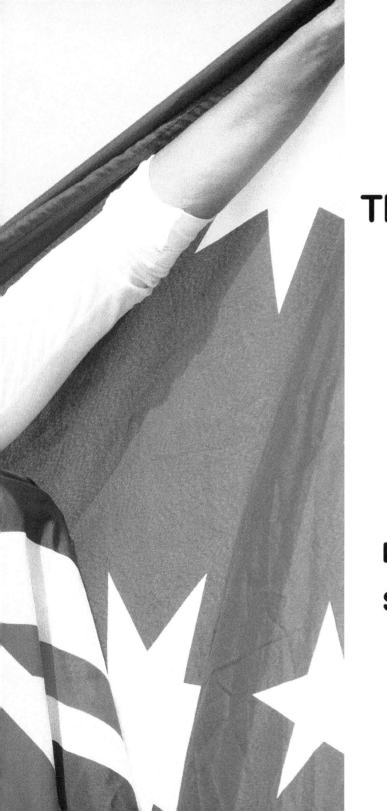

The name Australia was given to the country in 1824. It comes from the word 'terra australis incognita' that means 'unknown southern island'.

Australia is the smallest inhabited continent of the seven continents can also be considered the largest island in the world. In fact it is an island continent.

The first people to live in Australia were the 'Aborigines', and they've been there for approximately 60,000 years

Australia is really remote, that's why it's nicknamed 'down under' and because of this they've got loads of animals and plants that can't be found anywhere else in the world.

The highest mountain of Australia is Mount Kosciuszko with 2.228 metres or 7,310ft.

Ayers Rock also called 'Uluru' which is in the centre of the country is the largest alone standing rock in the world.

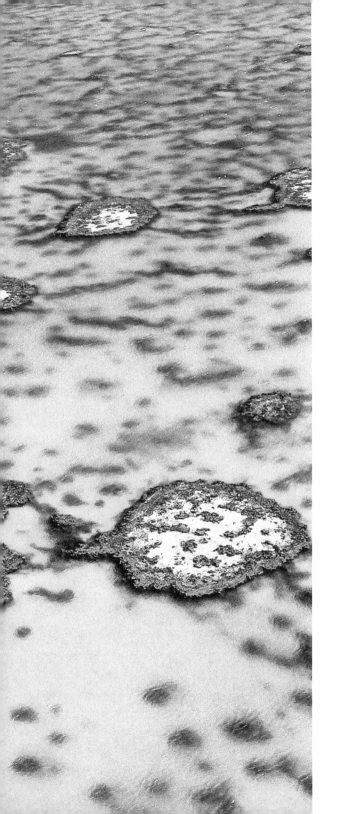

The Great Barrier Reef in Eastern Australia is the biggest coral reef in the world.

The tropical northern Australia is home to the world's largest species of salt water crocodiles.

Even though this is a big country, it doesn't have all that many people living there! There are about 3 people per square mile.

Today aborigines live in the desert areas of the Australian outback and they've learnt to survive under these harsh desert conditions.

Nearly a quarter of all the people that live there are born in other countries!

Can you believe that over 200 different languages and dialects are spoken in Australia of which 45 are indigenous!

Derby
Port Hedland
Carnarvon
WESTERN
AUSTRALIA
Perth
Albany
Adelaid

Australia is a commonwealth of the United Kingdom, which means that the head of state is none other than the Queen of England!

Australia has the largest cattle station in the world at 21,126 square miles (34,000km²).

They've invented loads of things including lawn mowers with engines, the Black Box on airplanes, smoke alarms and many more!

The longest fence in the world, referred to as the Dingo Fence, runs for 5,531 kilometres through Queensland and South Australia.

About 85% of
Australians live
within 50 km
from the coast

Australia has a lot to offer and you should visit the country soon and explore!

Visit

BABY PROFESSOR
EDUCATION KIDS

www.BabyProfessorBooks.com

to download Free Baby Professor eBooks
and view our catalog of new and exciting
Children's Books

Lightning Source UK Ltd.
Milton Keynes UK
UKHW051515150622
404459UK00004B/69